Multicultural Education

Éva Daragó

Multicultural Education

Multicultural Education through Language Learning

VDM Verlag Dr. Müller

Imprint

Bibliographic information by the German National Library: The German National Library lists this publication at the German National Bibliography; detailed bibliographic information is available on the Internet at
http://dnb.d-nb.de.
  Any brand names and product names mentioned in this book are subject to trademark, brand or patent protection and are trademarks or registered trademarks of their respective holders. The use of brand names, product names, common names, trade names, product descriptions etc. even without a particular marking in this works is in no way to be construed to mean that such names may be regarded as unrestricted in respect of trademark and brand protection legislation and could thus be used by anyone.

Cover image: www.purestockx.com

Published 2008 Saarbrücken

Publisher:
VDM Verlag Dr. Müller Aktiengesellschaft & Co. KG, Dudweiler Landstr. 125 a,
66123 Saarbrücken, Germany,
Phone +49 681 9100-698, Fax +49 681 9100-988,
Email: info@vdm-verlag.de
Zugl.: Veszprém, Pannon University, 2003

Produced in Germany by:
Reha GmbH, Dudweilerstrasse 72, D-66111 Saarbrücken
Schaltungsdienst Lange o.H.G., Zehrensdorfer Str. 11, 12277 Berlin, Germany
Books on Demand GmbH, Gutenbergring 53, 22848 Norderstedt, Germany

Impressum

Bibliografische Information der Deutschen Nationalbibliothek: Die Deutsche Nationalbibliothek verzeichnet diese Publikation in der Deutschen Nationalbibliografie; detaillierte bibliografische Daten sind im Internet über http://dnb.d-nb.de abrufbar.
  Alle in diesem Buch genannten Marken und Produktnamen unterliegen warenzeichen-, marken- oder patentrechtlichem Schutz bzw. sind Warenzeichen oder eingetragene Warenzeichen der jeweiligen Inhaber. Die Wiedergabe von Marken, Produktnamen, Gebrauchsnamen, Handelsnamen, Warenbezeichnungen u.s.w. in diesem Werk berechtigt auch ohne besondere Kennzeichnung nicht zu der Annahme, dass solche Namen im Sinne der Warenzeichen- und Markenschutzgesetzgebung als frei zu betrachten wären und daher von jedermann benutzt werden dürften.

Coverbild: www.purestockx.com

Erscheinungsjahr: 2008
Erscheinungsort: Saarbrücken

Verlag: VDM Verlag Dr. Müller Aktiengesellschaft & Co. KG, Dudweiler Landstr. 125 a,
D- 66123 Saarbrücken,
Telefon +49 681 9100-698, Telefax +49 681 9100-988,
Email: info@vdm-verlag.de
Zugl.: Veszprém, Pannon University, 2003

Herstellung in Deutschland:
Schaltungsdienst Lange o.H.G., Zehrensdorfer Str. 11, D-12277 Berlin
Books on Demand GmbH, Gutenbergring 53, D-22848 Norderstedt
Reha GmbH, Dudweilerstrasse 72, D-66111 Saarbrücken

ISBN: 978-3-639-01339-9

TABLE OF CONTENTS

- Chapter I -

THE NEED FOR MULTICULTURAL EDUCATION

"All human beings are born free and equal in dignity and rights."
(UN Declaration of Human Rights, 1948, Article 1)

I.1 Introduction

As our world is constantly changing, nationalities, cultures and languages are mixing, I have found it important to discuss a topic that is dealing with multiculturalism in language teaching. It is not only the duty of parents to draw children's attention to this fact but it is also the responsibility of teachers.

Nowadays we live in multicultural societies. The lifting of travel restrictions caused the flow of workforce from one country into another and the big gap between the living conditions results in the increase of the number of people escaping from poverty. Religious clashes, wars give rise to the appearance of shelter-seeking masses.

The problem lies in the fact that the rapid technological, political and economic changes are not followed by social-mental changes. A lot of things are happening to us that we cannot understand, that we cannot cope with. The results are exasperating: racist hostility, intolerance towards minorities, xenophobia, masses of refugees and asylum-seekers.

Living together is not an easy task for people therefore, we have to learn it and we have to teach it as well. Maybe the acceptance of otherness and the development of tolerance is the most difficult problem to solve. That's why I have chosen the sentence above, which is true and wise although, it is only theory and things rarely coincide with this in practice - we just have to look around in our world. I do not think that I am able to find a solution nevertheless, I am going to investigate and analyse some possibilities.

I.2. Definitions of some useful notions

- Culture: 1. "Anthropological or sociological culture: the attitudes, customs, and daily activities of a people, their ways of thinking, their values, their frames of reference."

     2. "History of civilization: includes geography, history, and achievements in the sciences, the social sciences, and the arts." (Joyce Merrill Valdes 1986:179)

- Multiculturalism: "having or blending many distinct cultures" (Clarence L. Barnhart - Robert K. Barnhart 1993)

- Multicultural society: "different cultural, national, ethnic, religious groups all living together within the same territory but not necessarily coming into contact with each other" (P. Brander - C. Cardenas - R. Gomes - M. Taylor - J. de Vicente Abad 1995:23)

- Tolerance: "a willingness to be patient toward people whose opinions or ways differ from one's own" (Clarence L. Barnhart - Robert K. Barnhart 1993)

- Intolerance: "lack of respect for practices or beliefs other than ones own" (P. Brander - C. Cardenas - R. Gomes - M. Taylor - J. de Vicente Abad 1995:30)

- Prejudice: "a judgement we make about another person or other people without really knowing them" (P. Brander - C. Cardenas - R. Gomes - M. Taylor - J. de Vicente Abad 1995:28)

- Discrimination: "is prejudice in action" (P. Brander - C. Cardenas - R. Gomes - M. Taylor - J. de Vicente Abad 1995:29)

- Stereotype: "shared beliefs or thoughts about a particular human group" (P. Brander - C. Cardenas - R. Gomes - M. Taylor - J. de Vicente Abad 1995:27)

I.3. Foreign language teaching and multicultural education

The question may arise: why is it important to introduce multiculturalism exactly into foreign language teaching?

The extent to which language, culture, and thought have influenced each other has been a matter of controversy for a long time. According to Kramsch "if language is seen as social practice, culture becomes the very core of language teaching" (Anne-Brit Fenner 2001:103). Foreign language teaching is one of the non-scientific subjects that requires thinking, imagination and association of ideas of students. Foreign language learning is not equivalent to the acquisition of grammatical rules and new words. Language teaching is a complex study, in which the freedom of thought is much more significant than for example, in mathematics or in chemistry. The teaching of culture must be an "aid to language learning rather than a hindrance" (Joyce Merrill Valdes 1986:vii). There is a constant tendency to make a comparison between students' own language, culture, society and the foreign conventions. For that very reason it is essential to make the children get in touch with the cultures of other countries as well. To achieve this purpose first they must become acquainted with their own surroundings and customs.

There are plenty of possibilities in foreign language teaching to accomplish this task. The modern language books are full of texts dealing with interesting topics. Nowadays the wide spread of advanced technology opens up new vistas in the whole education. Fortunately, the use of video, media and Internet is becoming more and more usual too. We must seize the opportunity to give an authentic representation to the students.

I.4. At what time should one start teaching multiculturalism?

If we really want to fulfil our purpose - that is to make students familiar with the concept of multiculturalism - we should begin introducing it into teaching as early as possible.

In primary schools, when one is young, it is less difficult to accept new ideas and ways of thinking. At this time students are more docile and more sensitive, perhaps also more susceptible to influence. For them a class is a community, a group of young children, ignoring racial and cultural differences. If they are acquainted with multiculturalism and the problems of living together rightly, they will be able to see things in their true colours in their future life. Of course, during the teaching, theories must be "wrapped up" in such a way that they will be perspicuous, moreover, interesting for every student. Telling stories, tales of other nations is a very good method for this but I am going to talk about it later in detail.

On the other hand, we may face up to some difficulties as well. To be able to tolerate otherness first we have to find our own social identity. We have to know how others see us and how we see others and ourselves. It is a kind of categorisation - sometimes even stereotyping - saying *I am a woman/ a teacher/ Hungarian/ Catholic* etc. Learners have to be guided to a "recognition of the cultural base of their own attitudes and behaviour" and after that they will be able to consider others "in a more favourable light" (Joyce Merrill Valdes 1986:2). Nevertheless, the young are sometimes not fully aware of their own personality, they cannot clarify their own thoughts and emotions. How could we expect them to evaluate different cultures, societies, lifestyles?

The other question that may arise is the problem of communicative competence, that is "being prepared for the unexpected" as well (Anne-Brit Fenner 2001: 18). At young age students are not on a right level of communicative competence that's why they are not able to communicate about these matters without restrictions. I think that they are not really prepared for this, considering either grammar or vocabulary. Of course, a kind of mental maturity is needed too.

An important question may be the nature of our teaching purposes: what are we learning for? There are different types of second language learning contexts. We can acquire a second language within the culture of the given language or within our own native culture where the second language is "an accepted lingua franca used for education, government, or business within the country (for example, learning English in the Philippines or India)" (Joyce Merrill Valdes 1986:34). Besides the age this factor must be considered as well.

It is also true that most of the students start learning English at secondary schools. By that time their way of thinking and opinion about the world is more or less formed. Therefore, it would be desirable to introduce language teaching and the teaching of English in every primary school - even in small villages.

Although these are very significant questions, in my opinion one of the biggest "enemies" of multicultural education is the lack of time. One of the characteristic features of our educational system is that it is very regulated, overstrained. Both teachers and learners are pressed to follow the textbooks and to acquire the material of a certain quantity; quality is often a matter of minor importance.

Some teachers tend to think that the problems of mankind cannot or must not be introduced into foreign language learning because they have nothing to do with each other, however, it is not true. Students are influenced by everything that is happening around them and we cannot exclude it from the classroom.

- Chapter II -

MULTICULTURAL EDUCATION IN LANGUAGE LEARNING: HISTORICAL REVIEW

II.1 "Knowing" a language

In this chapter I would like to analyse multicultural language teaching in the historical methods. I am going to investigate how much attention this aspect received, whether it was present at all or not.

Before doing it a very significant question has to be answered: What is foreign language learning, what does it include, what are the parts of it?

According to Wittgenstein "we don't know exactly what it means to know a language" (Anne-Brit Fenner 2001: 18). It is obviously more than the knowledge of the meaning and spelling of words. Do we *know* a language if we are conscious of the use of grammatical rules? Are we similar to native speakers if our language is totally acceptable and appropriate or is something still missing? Can we talk about the knowledge of foreign culture, thoughts, beliefs?

While we are trying to answer these questions we must not forget that there is no foreign language teaching without sociocultural content although, not all of the language teaching methods kept it in view.

II.2. Grammar translation method

Apart from some positive features it can be pointed out that the grammar translation method was not really favourable to multicultural education. This method, which appeared at the end of the 18th century, emphasized translation as the most important way of acquiring a foreign language. The lack of modern audio-visual equipment also hindered teachers in presenting the culture of the target country although it was not their aim at all.

The advantage of the "Prussian" method was the absorption of literature in foreign language teaching, since if we "teach language without teaching at the same time the culture in which it operates, we are teaching meaningless symbols" (Joyce Merrill Valdes 1986:123). Students had to read significant works of classical authors and these could transmit foreign culture to them to a certain extent. However, the odd and rarely used words may not have had a stimulating effect on students' learning pleasure.

At that time teachers concentrated mostly on the grammatical aspect of the language rather than the habits and lifestyle of the people living in that special country.

II.3. Direct method

This method caused radical changes in foreign language teaching during the turn of the century. It rejected the use of mother tongue and translation. The governing idea of teaching was "thinking in a foreign language" (Maximillian Berlitz) and the centre of it was the cultural-topical curriculum.

On the one hand, it was a great leap forward that students had the chance to become acquainted with the life and customs of foreign people and the history and geography of the target country. In this way learning was more interesting, moreover, they could make a comparison between the foreign and their own conditions.

On the other hand, these new techniques were too demanding for teachers and students as well. The children were not able to memorize so many new words and they became exhausted and dispirited after a while.

II.4. Reading method

This British method appeared around the 1920s. The essence of it was the so called extensive (synthetic) reading, by which teachers concentrated mostly on meaning and vocabulary rather than grammatical structures.

The disadvantage of this method was that it emphasized one skill only - that is reading skill - moreover the texts to be read by the children were not always properly selected.

Students had to learn 40-60 words for each lesson so their memory was exposed to a great "employment".

In spite of these facts the reading method was regarded as one of the best methods of making students familiar with foreign culture. While reading the texts they could seize the opportunity to enrich their vocabulary and satisfy their thirst for knowledge of other people and parts of the world at the same time.

II.5. Intensive method

Although the gradual improvement of trade, science and technology required the knowledge of languages even before the second world war, in the 1940s it became nearly unavoidable to be able to speak some foreign languages. At that time the intensive or the so called Army method brought some significant changes in foreign language learning. People wanted to attain to a minimal level within a short time and this special programme made it possible for them.

Nevertheless, it had its disadvantages too. Besides the continuous repetition and imitation of new words and whole sentences students did not have the time - or perhaps the energy - to immerse themselves in other important pieces of information about foreign people and countries. They apparently concentrated on efficiency at the expense of quality.

The benefit of the Army method was the new way of teaching, the appearance of teamwork. This kind of learning resulted in another psychological situation: people in the classroom depended on each other, they had to learn the concept of co-operation. This was a great step forward, since there is no multicultural education without a real community, a class, a group that can work and think together.

II.6. Audio-lingual method

This method of American origin became widespread in the 1940s. It was the first mass method of language teaching due to the technological improvement of that era and the discovery of new audio-devices like the tape-recorder. Soon the language laboratories appeared as well.

We may think that with the help of all these new inventions teachers had a free scope for multicultural education but that is not quite true. The tape-recorders were mostly used for different drills for example repetition of minimal pairs and memorization of sentence patterns whereas, it would have been suitable for presenting authentic texts, dialogues to the children, from which they would have been able to get some information about the users of the language they learn.

II.7. Audio-visual method

It was worked out in France by the C.R.E.D.I.F. in the 1960s but teachers can also benefit from it nowadays. The audio-visual method shows a great similarity to the previous - audio-lingual - method but in spite of this fact the former one sets out from the language as a complex, "living" thing. Three main language levels were distinguished:

- the first one was the level of everyday language with simple situations and the extensive use of audio-visual devices
- the second one was completed with reading and the analysis of the language and style of newspapers
- the third one included the use of some technical language as well

The centre of teaching was the *situation*, which is a very important part of multicultural education too. While students are performing some roles, they can practise the language and get some useful information about the culture and lifestyle of foreign people at the same time. In this way we can preserve both the entertaining and the instructive nature of the syllabus.

The followers of this method preferred stills (wallcharts, cartoons, pictures from magazines, brochures etc.) because the children could enter into the spirit of them, so they had the opportunity to obtain an insight into the everyday life and problems of those people. With the help of "bringing" foreign culture closer to students it could be less difficult to develop empathy and tolerance in them. Nowadays, in the midst of the great jump in technology, we have an easier job. There are plenty of different audio-visual devices at our disposal to fulfil our purpose.

II.8. The mentalist (cognitive) approach

Chomsky's new ideas about language and language learning undoubtedly stirred up the "stagnant water" of foreign language teaching in the 1960s. According to this view everything is in connection with the brain and language is a mental phenomenon, which can be acquired by the innate Language Acquisition Device (L.A.D.) that can be found in everyone of us. The so called *Cognitive Code Learning* was not equivalent to an automatic repetition of grammatical rules and new items. On the contrary, it demanded intelligent observation, thinking and creativity. That's why language learning is inconceivable without some social conditioning. Consequently this method was favourable to students having a rational disposition, being able to concentrate and see through difficult problems as well.

In my opinion this kind of language teaching was suitable for multicultural education because it pressed students to think instead of sitting and repeating words monotonously. The aim was to think in that foreign language - nearly "with the brain" of those foreign people. Certainly, that also requires a kind of mental maturity.

II.9. The humanistic approaches

II.9.1. Community Language Learning

This method was developed by C. A. Curran in the United States of America at the end of the 1960s. It set out from the fact that most students feel uncomfortable in the classroom, they are anxious and they regard learning as a kind of pressure. The basic principle was that by easing the tension they will achieve better results.

The classroom arrangement was very good from the point of view of multicultural education. Learners, who were called "clients", formed a circle so they could see each other's faces and gestures as well. By this way it is less difficult to manifest oneself and open up one's heart. This can create a more pleasant atmosphere, which is unfortunately often missing from present-day schools. The teachers, who were called "counsellors", were not in the centre of the classroom, they remained in the background. It follows from this that the "clients" could feel safe and free and because of the lack of teacher's control they were able to concentrate on their own thoughts and feelings. Moreover, they could pay attention to their class-mates as well.

Counselling Learning demanded the learning of working together and depending on each other. It is considered to be a significant advantage of Curran's method. This kind of teaching can give assistance to develop tolerance and the ability of accepting each other in the children.

II.9.2. TPR (Total Physical Response)

This method of J.J. Asher concentrated mainly on the beginner stage of language learning. It was an "action-centred" way of teaching: students had to obey the commands of the instructor, understanding was achieved through this technique. From the point of view of multicultural language learning it may not have been the best method. The postponement of speech and forcing children to listen during the lessons prevented them from exchanging their views and sharing their experiences with each other.

Although the humorous settings and the playful actions were able to make learning more interesting and to bring students closer to each other, Total Physical Response was not based on this. It is not enough for the children to do something, they also want to know why they are doing that exactly on that way. In my opinion learners did not have the possibility to express themselves, their own thoughts and personality.

II.9.3. Suggestopedia

"Down with the psychological and social barriers of learning!" - that could be the motto of a new foreign language teaching method that was developed by Georgij Lozanov in the 1960s and 1970s. It was called Suggestopedia. It was a student-centred method, whose main advantage was the creation of relaxed atmosphere and harmonious working conditions in the classroom. The whole teaching process was based on mutual confidence between the children and the teacher. By "bringing down the barriers" students were able to manifest themselves and express their thoughts without the fear of failure.

Role play was a significant technique of Suggestopedia. Learners had the chance to imagine themselves in somebody else's place and to understand the acts and feelings of others moreover, with the help of using fantasy names, they wore a kind of mask, which protected them at the same time.

Listening to classical music had more advantages as well. On the one hand, students became calmer and more impressionable, on the other hand, they could make themselves familiar with the musical culture of other parts of the world.

II.9.4. Silent Way

It is one of the humanistic methods that was developed by C. Gattegno. "Silent" in the name of this method refers to the role of the teacher, who did not intervene in the process of learning, or only if it was necessary. The students, who carried out the bulk of the work, formed a community. Being a member of the group and as a result of the peer correction children had to learn how to pay attention and listen to each other. This could develop the esprit de corps in other words, the feeling of belonging to a community.

In spite of these facts it was a considerably controlled method, which mostly concentrated on good pronunciation and intonation but the vocabulary it taught was rather shallow. Considering all the facts in my opinion it was not the best way for multicultural language teaching.

II.10. Communicative language learning

At the beginning of the 1970s sweeping changes appeared not only in foreign language teaching but in other fields of life as well. External relations between the countries became stronger, the flow of migrant workers became more and more significant. Nations came closer to each other. Naturally, these processes gave rise to important events in foreign language learning too, and a new method appeared, called Communicative Language Learning. It regarded language as a real means of communication, almost a working tool. Language was also said to be the channel of expressing our thoughts and feelings, not only an information-sending device.

Was this method favourable to multicultural education? There are several advantages that I would like to mention. One of them are the teaching techniques: the role plays, simulations, language games and drama techniques are all supporting devices for teachers who aim at developing tolerance and empathy in children. There is always an information gap, which is a desire to communicate, and the more students communicate with each other, the easier it will be to accept the others' opinions and ways of thinking.

The big variety of classroom techniques (individual work, pair work, group work) also serves this purpose. The method is undoubtedly characterized by learner centeredness and communication centeredness, which are favourable for multicultural education. The use of authentic materials, like newspaper articles, during the teaching process is thought to be an advantage of the Communicative approach as well. It can be also mentioned that students had an opportunity to contribute to classroom learning with their own experiences, therefore, the topics of the curriculum got "closer" to them, it resulted in a more intimate atmosphere.

II.11. Summary of the historical review, conclusion

If we go through the most important foreign language teaching approaches from the 18th century onwards, it can be pointed out that the palette of the methods is very colourful. There were approaches that did not really favour multicultural education (for example Grammar Translation method) and there were a lot among the methods that had modern techniques, innovations that caused radical changes in language teaching, which were also favourable for multicultural learning (for example the use of audio-lingual devices, the appearance of learner centred ways of teaching or the spread of new, interesting classroom solutions like drama techniques and role plays).

Considering all the facts, due to the process of the development of different foreign language teaching methods, the circumstances of multicultural education became more and more advantageous. The question may arise: Why is it nowadays more and more important to talk about multiculturalism and to introduce this kind of teaching into the classroom?

The present-day foreign language teaching has a big advantage: it is not only aimed at teaching the language itself but teachers feel themselves bound to share some useful pieces of information about different countries and people with the students. Unfortunately, these data are often limited to the ones about the target country only. But a plenty of significant and sometimes very sad events happen all over the world that would deserve some attention. Nowadays, when everybody tends to mind his own business and does not care for the others, when we gradually become alienated from each other, there would be a big need for talking about this matter. Hopefully, the future foreign teaching methods will pay more and more attention to multiculturalism and will find a solution to some still burning questions of today.

- Chapter III -

HUMAN AND NON-HUMAN FACTORS REQUIRED IN MULTICULTURAL EDUCATION AND LANGUAGE LEARNING

III.1. Introduction

In this chapter I would like to concentrate on the conditions that are necessary when we have the aim to introduce multicultural language learning in a school. These terms can be classified into two big groups:

1. Non-human factors

    → classroom conditions

    → teaching aids, devices

2. Human factors

    → qualities of the teacher

    → qualities of the students in the class

Before I start collecting and analysing all of these terms I would like to mention at the outset that it will be a "perfect" state that I am going to outline. Of course, not all of these factors can be carried out in a classroom, nevertheless, we have to try to accomplish as much as possible. It needs attention, a lot of time, patience and last but not least a lot of money.

Unfortunately, the organisation of multicultural education is still in its infancy in Hungary. The gradual opening towards the outside world, which demands getting acquainted with foreign cultures, charges more expenses to the state and shifts more responsibility onto the teachers. Culture is a comprehensive notion, which includes sociology, musical culture, traditions and habits, communicational culture as well, and the enumeration could be continued. Peoples, countries and the whole world are many-sided and those who have undertaken the task of introducing children into it obviously have to face plenty of difficulties. At the age of the revolution of exchanging information it is almost impossible to comprise every minute detail but if we manage to develop tolerance in the students, we can say that we have already achieved important results.

The first and inevitable task is to make it possible for children of different ethnic groups and with various cultural backgrounds to go to the same school with the others. In other words, we have to avoid segregation in education because that could be the source of lots of troubles later. Education is actually the first phase of the integration of the minorities into the society. Of course it does not mean a kind of assimilation through which these people have to abandon their own traditions and habits, on the contrary, we have to help them to preserve their peculiarities and values. This process can be favourable to the minorities to join forces and keep pace with the majority because the growing of the gap between them is giving cause for alarm.

Integration in practice is not so simple as it sounds to be theoretically. We have to face plenty of problems, conflicts and frustration, as living together is never free from prejudices and the manifestation of intolerance. Nevertheless, it would be more expedient if children were acquainted with reality right from the beginning because the occurring difficulties are still manageable at that time. If the solution of "excluding" schools was accepted, a lot of children would grow up with the experience that human beings are not equal to each other and somebody is superior, the others are inferior. Unfortunately, too many adults can call this view their own, moreover, they hand it down to the younger generation as well. That's why the responsibility of teachers is very significant in this question.

III.2. The non-human factors of multicultural education

Non-human factors is a cover-term for the arrangements that depend partly on organizational ability, partly on financial means. Everything belongs to here what makes education easier, comfortable, more interesting and spectacular. First of all, it would be very useful to introduce foreign language teaching in every school, even in the villages. It would be pleasing if students had the chance to choose between more languages but the teaching of English is nearly inevitable today. Children cannot be deprived of this right just because they were born in a less developed region of the country. The knowledge of foreign languages is almost essential nowadays, at least it makes our future life and prosperity less difficult. We can only talk about further duties if this primary condition is realized.

III.2.1. Classroom conditions

While I was talking about the humanistic methods I have emphasized the importance of peaceful surroundings and pleasant atmosphere. This is not only the requirement of multicultural teaching but of every kind of educational situation. The adequate surroundings may help a lot both the teachers and the pupils with the learning process. We should provide a peaceful and aesthetically satisfying environment for them, as it has a lot of advantages. On the one hand, the participants take delight in studying, on the other hand, it may "discharge creative energy" in the children (Kahánné Goldman Leonóra - Poór Zoltán 1999:99). Fortunately, the number of such educational institutions is constantly growing but still there are plenty of schools with bare - often crumbling - walls and without any materials or devices that could make studying not only bearable but even enjoyable. No wonder, that children do not find great pleasure in learning under such circumstances.

Unfortunately, a typical, traditional classroom arrangement does not favour multicultural education at all. Students are sitting with their back to each other, very often they cannot hear the teacher in spite of the fact that he or she is standing in the centre, in front of the class as a director or a leader of the group. It is the worst solution when he or she has to stand on a platform like an omnipotent power because it immediately infuriates animosity. It would be better to form a circle in the room so that everybody could see each other's facial expressions, gestures and movements because they often tell us more than words. When students are accustomed to this arrangement perhaps it will be less difficult for them to establish relations in their future lives and to express their opinions frankly. The freedom of movement is very important for students, as well as for the teacher. They should always have the chance to contact with each other. By that way children learn how to give voice to their own thoughts and how to take the consequences of that.

Besides the arrangement the decoration of the classroom is another significant factor. It has to be fashioned in compliance with the students age, maturity, interest and the teaching aim too, therefore, it is not an easy task to design it. It would be useful if it was brought or made by the children themselves. The teachers can distribute the task of making such decoration among the students for homework or during the lesson. It is better if that is part of our lesson plan because it breaks monotony, develops creative instinct and the feeling of belonging to a community and that of depending on each other in the students, who are working in small groups. It can be an efficient means of persuading children to talk on a language lesson, even those ones who did not want or did not dare to use the foreign language in practice. While preparing the decoration we should avoid one-sided solutions, in other words, it has to reflect the way of thinking, emotions and opinions of everybody who took a share in making it. The more aspect it has, the more suitable it is from a multicultural point of view. We should always let the students express themselves, that is their own personalities. The treasure of the means at our disposal is inexhaustible. We can use pictures, photographs, drawings or charts, which may be displayed on the wall. Making or collecting dioramas and other kinds of realia may also be an exciting challenge for children and not only for the younger ones. The above mentioned activities have three main purposes, namely:

- to develop students' communicative and creative abilities
- to produce a pleasant environment, in which studying is not a force but a delight
- to make learners familiar with the concept of togetherness, through which they get to know themselves and the others too.

These complex activities have a big advantage: they can be carried out without significant financial expenditure. The situation is not so encouraging in the case of the devices that could facilitate the learning process.

III.2.2 Teaching aids, devices

To be able to introduce multicultural education in a country it would be necessary to provide equal chances for each school to be able to teach under the same conditions. The amount and distribution of the money expended on education is always a matter of great importance. The situation is the same in the case of teaching aids. What kind of devices are we talking about and how can they promote multicultural learning?

The range of such aids is again almost immense. First of all the different course books, workbooks, activity books should be mentioned. The palette of them is by no means so deficient as it used to be a few decades ago. Due to the new ways of thinking and new approaches an opportunity presents itself for every one of us to find exactly the book we need. Fortunately, the multicultural aspect is more often presented in the contemporary language books as well but I am going to talk about this fact later on.

Although language books are going to be more and more useful and interesting, the teachers have to complete them with other kinds of materials to be able to avoid shallowness and monotony. A very important principle of selecting materials is authenticity. According to Little and Singleton an authentic material is "created to fulfil some social purpose in the language community in which it was produced" (Anne-Brit Fenner 2001:84). We can make a distinction between "educational" authentic and "didactic" authentic materials:

→ "educational" authentic: published for the speakers of the target language for educational purposes

→ "didactic" authentic: made by the teacher who will use them

(Zoltán Poór: Technology in Teaching English as a Foreign Language)

Authenticity is important because with the help of it students can meet reality, real, everyday situations of life, which are not distorted. Sometimes they can learn more from a facial expression or a kind of intonation than from the whole text. It is not accidental that even the old Greeks and Latin people used such materials during the teaching process.

There are more criteria that must be taken into consideration in order to select the most appropriate material for each lesson and for each group of learners. On the one hand, it has to suit the requirements of teaching a foreign language:

- it must fit for the level of the students
- it must include neither a lot of new words nor too difficult grammatical structures
- it has to be of adequate length and of correct language.

On the other hand, it has to be suitable from a multicultural point of view as well. The materials must be intelligible and interesting to be able to serve as a motivation for the students. They may bring up some difficult, thought-provoking issues, by which the teacher can make the learners reflect on those matters. As I have mentioned, before it is inevitable to marshal different viewpoints and opinions at the same time because the aids serve as a means of expressing the cultural diversities of a given nation.

We can enumerate plenty of authentic materials (the list is not intended to be exhaustive):

- any kind of books, booklets
- newspapers, magazines
- leaflets, brochures
- albums, catalogues
- television programmes
- video guides
- radio programmes
- posters, maps, photos, charts etc.

The aids can be grouped as print, video and audio materials. The former one is probably the most available among them. To be able to present the latter ones (video and audio materials) the technical demands must be provided as well. At the age of the technological progress it is necessary for every educational institution to dispose of overhead projectors, televisions, videos (perhaps cameras), radio cassette recorders and naturally computers. Unfortunately, the accessibility to such equipment raises difficulties even at universities not to mention small primary schools.

Besides video and radio programmes Internet is gaining more and more ground nowadays, as a means of connecting people from different parts of the world. Its main role in multicultural education is to ensure the chance of interaction between peers. Its main advantage over videos and radios is the possibility of immediate feedback and of bilateral relations. It gives an opportunity for social interaction, "the means of transmitting cultural and historical knowledge" (Garton 1992:11). Hopefully Internet will spread widely in the future in Hungary too.

An additional but very important group of the teaching aids is *realia*. Realia has two main types: objects from universal reality (like a piece of furniture) and objects typical to the target language culture. The treasury of such things is enormous. Here are some examples that can be ranked among them:

- national costumes
- flags
- coins
- recipes
- boxes of food
- tickets etc.

With the help of such objects students can make themselves familiar with the habits, traditions and everyday life of people from other countries in addition, they can compare it to their own culture and they can learn a lot from this comparison. The benefit of using realia while teaching is that children can see and touch the things in reality, about which they would otherwise only read or hear.

All these teaching aids and devices that I have listed in the foregoing are aimed at promoting multicultural education. Teachers use them with a view to bringing foreign culture closer to the students and making learning deeply interesting. However, it is not worth much without the teacher's proper attitude to multiculturalism and the right way of looking at things. That's why the teacher's personality is playing a very significant role in the teaching process.

III.3. The human factors

Societies and social interaction are based on the relationship between human beings and the way of social interaction is communication. Therefore, there was, there is and there will be always a constant claim to study languages. Communication is often taking place between people with totally different cultural, social, ethnic or religious background. For this reason it is not enough to *know* a foreign language but we also have to know *how* to communicate. Similarly to the language, it also has to be taught to the children although, culture is a very nebulous concept with as many interpretations as many people there are on the world. The "way of doing and interpreting things is not natural (i.e. the only possible way) but cultural" (Michael Byram - Manuel Tost Planet 2000:189). Consequently, the human factors, the person of the teacher are not negligible at all.

III.3.1. Qualities of the teacher

Our world is like a perpetuum mobile, being in endless motion and continually developing. It is getting more and more difficult to find our way in the era of the technological boom and information deluge. Children have to be prepared for this task and it is not only the duty of the parents but of the teachers as well. Students - especially young children - are often imitating adults, they consider them as models and they make their views their own. It follows from this that the "head" of the class has to furnish a good example of behaving in this world so that the younger generation can step in the footsteps of him or her. This needs an adequate attitude and way of thinking on the part of the educators, therefore, the teacher's personality is of crucial importance.

By the way of introduction I would like to enumerate the most significant characteristic features of a teacher that are very important in the case of "traditional" language education but indispensable in the case of multicultural language teaching. As educators partly substitute for parents in the class, this profession means an educational and welfare work at the same time. The primary task of a teacher is to create his or her own way of thinking and opinion about the world and to believe it to be true. If they are not sure of their own right, they will not be able to persuade anybody of it. Naturally, it does not mean that the teacher must not be open for other opinions too.

The second important factor is achieving communicative competence, in other words, the teachers must be capable of expressing their own thoughts. Being a foreign language teacher the proper knowledge of the given language (vocabulary, grammar, intonation, idioms etc.) is essential: his or her language must be appropriate and acceptable in every situation. But that is only one part of the demands that need to be satisfied.

While teaching a foreign language teachers should incorporate as much factual knowledge about the target country into the curriculum as possible. That requires on the one hand a general education and expertness in the matters of life, on the other hand a considerable amount of information about the given nation in other words, sociocultural competence. Educators have to possess factual material about the geographical, social, economical data, culture, traditions, politics, arts and habits of the target community. They must be fully aware of the conversational customs, conventions too (for example what is polite or impolite, what passes for humorous and what is considered to be insulting) but that already belongs to the field of sociolinguistics. However, it is not enough yet. They must also arouse the students' interest and demand to become acquainted with all these facts.

There are some common features that must be characteristic of every educator, teaching either a foreign language or other subjects:

→ They have to be helpful so that students can turn to them at any time.

→ They must be aware of the importance of tolerance towards otherness and they have to accept diversity but avoid negative discrimination among the students.

→ Patience and empathy are also essential concomitants of multicultural education, teachers should always show understanding towards the children.

→ Although nobody is alike and every child comes from a different social, religious, cultural or family background, teachers must treat them without prejudices and favouritism.

→ An intelligent and proper attitude to culture as such is also required. A sophisticated EFL teacher, while introducing students to a certain culture, must also encourage them to maintain their own cultural identity, however, teachers should refrain from looking on their own culture as superior or almighty. Although "it is as impossible to escape from one's own culture as it is to get out of one's own skin" (Joyce Merrill Valdes 1986:153), other civilizations can also offer us precious things, we just have to select them carefully. Educators should also keep away from judging a culture but they can compare them. With the help of this comparative approach they can "provide a double perspective but not to evaluate to see which is better" (Michael Byram - Mamuel Tost Planet 2000:189). None of the civilizations is better or worse that the others, they are simply different. If we can make students understand this view, they will have the chance to learn a lot from these comparisons and hopefully they will be able to turn it to their advantage in their future life.

→ A good teacher always provides free scope for self-expression. The only way of discovering what is inside the students is to let them expound their own point of views and opinions frankly.

→ Since the teacher is the leader of a community, certain clashes and conflicts are inescapable. Therefore, he or she has to have the ability to solve the arising problems, moreover, the ability to prevent the formation of awkward situations. We can rarely find any community in which there was no stratification, expulsion, clique-formation and similar difficulties. Discrimination bears hostility and hostility causes disorder, which prevents the group from working well. The teacher's task is to handle these issues in a proper way, by setting the children a good example, which they can follow.

→ A teacher's profession is very complex, including different abilities and skills. What kind of roles does a teacher have in the classroom? There are several roles that can be mentioned.

A teacher can be for example:

• a guide (giving instructions, organizing)

• a controller (monitoring)

• an assessor (evaluating)

• a prompter (encouraging, suggesting)

• a participant (e.g. teacher-student pair work)

• a resource (providing information)

• a tutor (counselling)

• an investigator (looking for new ways, methods out of the classroom)

• an educator (transmitting morals, serving as a model)

These roles can be found in the personality of a versatile teacher but it is detrimental when one of them dominates while it is repressing the others. Thus, for the sake of an effective educational and welfare work they must be counterbalanced.

It is very useful from a multicultural point of view if students have the opportunity to meet some and native visitors from the target country in the language lesson. On the one hand, they can get acquainted with the "real" foreign accents, intonation and language use, moreover, with the rooted expressions, gestures, movements (the non-verbal channel of expression) of that given person as well. This is of great importance with a view to foreign language learning, since language is taught as a means of communication and exchanging information. On the other hand, pupils can make themselves familiar with the views, thoughts, opinions of a native person. It may be quite illuminating to compare the way they are thinking about themselves with our expectations or prejudices. Besides that the subject of stereotyping might be brought up as well. "It is very natural to associate a people - in appearance, manners, and possibly thought patterns - with the language they speak" (Joyce Merrill Valdes 1986:2) but we must not expect all members of a culture to fit the generality. People often tend to pigeonhole others, for example *the Scots are avaricious, the Germans are meticulous or the Italians are bohemian*. Well now, it may be an interesting question to be analysed whether they are really suited for these categories or not.

As the teachers have always an effect on their pupils, either deliberately or involuntary, it is required on the part of them to possess all of the characteristic features that I have listed so far in order to be good teachers and to be able to achieve their purposes. They are playing a kind of role every day when they step out in front of the class. Their life is like an "open book", reflecting their daily mood, joys and sorrows. If the role that they are playing is not genuine, children will immediately see through them. Nevertheless, teachers are human beings too, who sometimes simply cannot conceal their feelings, their likes and dislikes. In spite of this fact they must try to be objective in any kind of situation and perhaps in this way they can overcome their prejudices. There may be often a doubt in them whether they are behaving properly or not, in this case the colleagues are playing a significant role in emboldening or discouraging them.

If teachers want to meet all these requirements and carry out the tasks that I have enumerated, they have to prepare for fighting it out. It demands a lot of energy, time and work, boundless enthusiasm and steadfastness. They have to keep abreast of the times in our constantly changing world. They must be well up in psychology too, to be able to handle the coming up conflicts and problems. In other words, multicultural language teaching demands a lot but offers a lot at the same time. If we are doing our work conscientiously, we will reap our reward: a new, tolerant and open generation, whose members are able to accept each other without respect to cultural, religious, ethnic or social background.

III.3.2. Syllabus planning

To implement an intercultural approach would require some curricular revision for the courses. A significant issue is that how much of the core curriculum can be devoted to the teaching of culture: "intercultural activities and courses must be given the same importance in the curriculum as all other language activities" (Joyce Merrill Valdes 1986:157). During the teaching of a foreign language teachers can adopt three kinds of methods to help the students acquire the language and a proper way of thinking about the world at the same time. These are the following:

→ cognitive methods

→ practical methods

→ methods related to attitude

(Kahánné Goldman Leonóra - Poór Zoltán 1999:108)

The cognitive approach aims at transmitting some knowledge about other nations, cultures (not exclusively about the target country). As this factual material is brought closer to the children, they will be able to accept otherness more easily. Teaching of practical communication is directed towards the attainment of such cultural customs and conventions that facilitate students' position when they would like to get in touch with people from other countries. Methods related to behaviour tend to develop tolerance in the children and a kind of open attitude towards otherness without prejudices.

Besides all of these methods a carefully prepared syllable of teaching a foreign language involves some general principles as well:

• foreign language teaching has to ensure students the opportunity for developing their writing, reading, speaking and listening abilities in other words, both the productive and receptive skills

• the students should make themselves familiar with the target language culture through the acquisition of the given language

• teachers have to find a way to help pupils make a comparison between the target culture and their own way of life and through this they also have the possibility to become immersed in their own culture more deeply

• children's curiosity and empathy must be raised towards the people living in the foreign country

• teachers have to develop the necessary abilities in the students in order to make them able to get and systemize the information they need

While drawing up the schedule of teaching a foreign language there are several angles that must be taken into consideration. Students' age, interest, previous knowledge and abilities are all of great importance. Teachers also have to bear students skills and knowledge in mind, which they will need for succeeding in the new culture in the future. Learners - since they are members of the new generation - must be prepared for finding their place in our world, which is changing with more and more increased speed.

A syllable has to comprise the outlined fields and topics of the course, which the class is going to deal with, but they must be included as a result of a careful selection. The most frequently occurring thematic fields are for example:

→ geographical data

→ historical data

→ social life

→ politics, public affairs

→ facts connected with everyday life

- meals

- time-table, daily life

- clothing, fashion

- national holidays

- public transportation

- shopping etc.

→ arts (music, literature, architecture, movies…)

Each of the topics can give a good opportunity to broaden not only our vocabulary but our horizons and knowledge about the given culture as well. By this way the possible problems and conflicts may be pointed out and students may try to find the reasons for them or perhaps they might come up with some solutions. The following two situations may serve as examples:

1. *While examining the society and historical life of the two Irelands the teacher draws pupils' attention to the conflicts between Roman Catholics and Protestants in Northern Ireland, which unfortunately give rise to serious clashes even nowadays. After the teacher has explained the antecedents, the class tries to analyse the situation together and everybody has the chance to expound their views about the issue of religious inconsistency.*

2. *Concerning the social and historical life of the United States of America the position of the Blacks has always been of great importance and it has an impact on present life too. In connection with this the problem of racist hostility and discrimination can be discussed together from different point of views. What do children think about racialism and what could be the possible solutions to it?*

Naturally all of these situations and questions can be taken to refer to other nations and parts of the world. For instance the first problem can pertain to the war between the Palestinians and the Jews in Asia. However, some conclusions can be drawn regarding our own country and society too. Unfortunately, the issue of discrimination can be applied to Hungary as well in connection with the Gipsy population.

III.3.3. Qualities of students in the class

During their career teachers may come across many types of learners. The characteristic features of students depend on a lot of factors, which may differ from child to child. Their age, previous knowledge, intellectual skills, the level of motivation or anxiety, their expectations about the teaching material can all exercise influence on their education. According to Hanson, Silver and Strong four types of learners can be denominated:

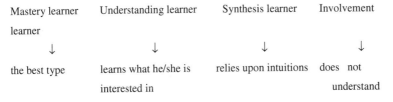

Mastery learner	Understanding learner	Synthesis learner	Involvement learner
↓	↓	↓	↓
the best type	learns what he/she is interested in	relies upon intuitions	does not understand

When all these types of learners come across each other in a class, it is a hard fight to weld them together into a real community, nevertheless, teachers must make every effort to do it. The importance of peer group education is the main point of multicultural teaching and although students might differ a lot, their class is a "collectivity in which the members share some common characteristics" (Domino Council of Europe 1996:8). Teachers must base on these shared qualities to be able to create a unity. When children find themselves in a totally unknown, new situation, naturally, they have some fears and prejudices. In order to be able to overcome such difficulties, they have to get to know each other; the means of this is the "cross-cultural communication" (Rogers) by which they will be able to accept otherness through becoming acquainted with other views as well. When this first phase is accomplished, the second step may come, namely, persuading children to work and think together as a real group. After that students' attention can be directed to wider perspectives, to different people from other parts of the world.

The student-exchange programmes may have a considerable effect on learners communicative competence - cross-cultural communication as well - and way of thinking. Through meeting native children in their natural surroundings a good opportunity presents itself for them to improve their language knowledge and familiarize themselves with the habits, beliefs and way of life in the target country at the same time. There are some useful programmes on international level to give assistance to schools to carry out these plans, for example, SOCRATES, which aims at promoting the intercultural dimension of education and the mobility of teaching staff and students.

While the teachers set it as an aim to give a chance to the students to meet children from other countries, they also have to consider the problem of social distance. The expression refers to "the cognitive and affective proximity of two cultures which come into contact within an individual" (Joyce Merrill Valdes 1986:39). If there is a significant dissimilarity between the cultures - for example, in the case of a European and an Asian country - it is the teacher's task to bridge this wide gap with the help of some activities serving this purpose, like sending "audio letters" or "video letters" to each other.

Second language learning does often mean - in some respects - the acquisition of a second identity. Acculturation, that is "the process of becoming adapted to a new culture" (Joyce Merrill Valdes 1986:33) is a complex process, which is beset with many pitfalls. The gradual adaptation to the target language and culture does not mean that we have to forsake our own native language identity. According to H. Douglas Brown the first phase of the acquisition is the speaking of an "interlanguage". At the initial phase motivation is especially strong and a great deal of language learning must be accomplished. If this period passes without reaching a certain threshold of communicative competence, learners may become "stuck" at the level of "functional competence" (Joyce Merrill Valdes 1986:21). There is another categorization that I would like to mention in connection with acculturation.

William R. Acton and Judith Walker de Felix:

1. Tourist: the phase in which the new culture is almost totally inaccessible, learners draw extensively on first language strategies and resources

2. Survivor: the stage of functional language (similar to pidgin) and functional understanding of a culture

3. Immigrant: the phase reached by most literate people who spend an extended period of time working or living in a foreign culture

4. Citizen: the stage that is almost at the level of the native speaker

(Joyce Merrill Valdes 1986:22)

In order to enable students to reach these phases, teachers have to select the proper classroom applications, techniques and activities very carefully. There are plenty of techniques for teaching a foreign language but good techniques for teaching culture and a foreign language at the same time are not so easy to find.

- Chapter IV -
CLASSROOM APPLICATIONS

IV.1. Introduction

A lot of linguists are interested in theories, new ways and ideas about foreign language teaching but unfortunately, sometimes there is a tendency to neglect the classroom itself, which is the place of plotting and putting everything into practice, where theories are made or broken, found to be either productive or useless. After the certain values and behaviour patterns have been determined, one must specify the most effective way of transmitting them. In foreign language classes the cultural component is often included in conversations, reading material, writing topics or listening exercises. "Since one must read, speak, or write about *something* and listen to something, why should not that *something* have a cultural content?" (Joyce Merrill Valdes 1986:121) The experimentation over long years resulted in a wide variety of paths to follow; techniques, approaches, methods, all are to be found along these paths and are adaptable to any language classroom. Although it would be next to impossible to enumerate all of these techniques, at least one may try to determine the most important fields and materials to be applied.

IV.2. Project work

Project work can be defined as a series of carefully planned and negotiated, multi-skill activities that are carried out in a co-operative, creative atmosphere with the aim to produce something tangible that has got a real function in real life. Project work is student-centred, encouraging children's spontaneous expression and developing their use of the foreign language with native speakers as well. Since it is based on group work, it contributes to the learners' social development and it has the advantage of integrating language skills with cultural topics or themes. Projects can be grouped as:

→ "paper" projects

→ "audio" projects

→ "video" projects

→ voiced "paper" projects

The alternatives of their application are inexhaustible, for example:

1. *writing postcards*

2. *making video guides of a town*

3. *making a comparison between the foreign and one's own television programmes*

4. *constructing "voiced albums"* etc.

Such tasks tend to increase solidarity and the sense of responsibility towards others in the classroom and they contribute to developing students' communicative competence and background knowledge at the same time.

IV.3. Literature and drama in the classroom: "Literature represents the personal voice of a culture" (Anne-Brit Fenner 2001:16)

Until the 1970s or the first half of the 1980s the integration of literary texts and literature into teaching English as a foreign language was rather neglected. Reading and listening are said to be non-productive, receptive skills but on reflection, one has to admit that while interpreting a text we already produce something, namely, our own meaning. According to Vachek learners study a foreign language "with constant regard to the history (economic, political, and cultural) of the people using that language" (Anne-Brit Fenner 2001:81) and a well-chosen literary text - as a kind of "ideological bridge" between the cultures - can initiate discussions about these topics, moral values and cultural similarities or differences as well. While the class is working with these texts, there is a constant contact between the learner and the text, the members of the class, and the teacher and the learners themselves. A literary text provides motivation, and information about culture, has richer semiotics, and multiplicity of meaning, moreover, it may function as a model for learners' own text production. There are several language tasks - both oral and written - that may follow the discussion of literary texts, for example:

1. *transformation*
2. *putting lines in the correct order*
3. *essay writing*
4. *comparing it to everyday dialogue*
5. *performing the text*

The last point is of great importance. The main aim of drama is "to make people react personally to another person's verbal sensibility" (Anne-Brit Fenner 2001:49). Nevertheless, it is not so simple as it sounds to be, because different cultures speak differently, considering the loudness, turn-taking, politeness-formulae, different expressions in certain situations. In spite of this fact, acting provides great pleasure and delight and develops students' creativity and self-confidence. There are plenty of texts and possibilities of their application at our disposal, like:

1. *Dealing with the Theatre of absurd and the texts of Ionescu or Beckett the teacher may shed light upon the importance of communication and raise the question: why and how can language alienate people?*

Audio and video applications may contribute to making role plays and drama teaching even more interesting and useful. By this way an opportunity presents itself to record and later to discuss these materials but through the analysis one should avoid evaluation because in that case the teacher may influence learners' opinion.

IV.4. The press, newspapers

Newspapers can be also used as vehicles for teaching a foreign language but again with a significant cultural focus. The press is a many-sided resource of teaching materials; there are cultural, political, social, economical news, letters to the editor, horoscopes, cartoons, interviews etc. in the newspapers. The class can discuss its vocabulary, style, as well as the opinions and views about the world, they can compare them to their own native press too. But the newspaper is not easy to teach from, it puts a considerable strain on the teacher, whose guidance is necessary, since there is so much cultural interference and language difficulty. However, it also requires intensive work and active participation on the students' part.

IV.5. Role plays, games

We all have opinions, ideas and feelings about the world around us that we would like to share but sometimes it is rather difficult to talk about them. These activities help us to express ourselves openly. Role plays and games give good examples of the effective teaching techniques, which offer pleasure, develop creative power and communicative competence and focus attention on cross-cultural aspects at the same time. While performing a role play, "students take on the parts of typical members of host and native cultures" (Joyce Merrill Valdes 1986:151) and it makes easier to accept otherness. I would like to list some examples as well:

1. *Euro-rail "A la carte": This activity is about looking at prejudices using an everyday situation: travelling together on a train. The teacher has to give brief descriptions about the fellow passengers (e.g. a Serbian soldier, an African woman, a Swiss financial broker, a young artist who is HIV positive, a skinhead from Sweden, a Roma man...) and students should choose the three people they would most like to travel with and the three they would least like to travel with. Then they compare their choices and the reasons for them.*

2. *Dear friend...: Students should write a personal letter to another member of the group about a particular issue, for example, about being a member of a minority, racism, injustice etc. After that the others may write replies as well.*

3. *Guess who is coming to dinner?: Four learners are playing the role of a white family. There is a mother, a father, and a daughter, who is bringing home a black boyfriend. The father is for racism, the mother is against it.*

4. *Knysna Blue: Music is an excellent way to bring us closer to other cultures, but it can also be a carrier of stereotypes and biases. The teacher plays some music to the class and they have to try and guess where it comes from.*

5. *First impressions: It is very easy to make false assumptions about people when we meet them first. The teacher has to select pictures of people who have interesting/different/striking... faces or appearance. Students write down their first impressions and pass the sheet on to the next person. Then they compare their opinions.*

(The examples are taken from All different/all equal, pages: 78, 70, 87, 106, 83.)

- Chapter V -

ANALYSIS OF COURSEBOOKS

V.1. Introduction

"There are no perfect textbooks which completely and successfully integrate language instruction with cultural components" (Joyce Merrill Valdes 1986:160). Nevertheless, there are significant factors and guidelines on the basis of which teachers can improve upon textbook selection. In this chapter I would like to analyse some language books from a multicultural point of view. I intended to examine the exercises, the examples and their cultural context, and whether the photographs and illustrations - if any - are culturally related or not. I also meant to analyse the texts and dialogues and the use of authentic materials. The books are selected from different eras: from the 1960s, 70s, 80s, 90s, and from the present of English language teaching as well. So there may be a lot of differences and changes that can be pointed out.

V.2. Analysis of the books

1. The sixties

I have examined three books from the 60s:

- J. Smolska - J. Rusiecki (1966) English for Everyone

Warsaw

- L.G. Alexander (1967) First things First

Longman, London

- G. Broughton (1968) Success with English - The Penguin Course

Penguin Books

The first issue that can be stated in general is the absence of intercultural aspect. There are commonplace, "prefabricated" dialogues and texts in the books about everyday matters (for example *In the mountains* or *Tony and the goldfish* in *Success with English*) and unfortunately we can find no - or very few - authentic materials among them. The texts provide little background information for the learners and only about the target country, so there are no data about other foreign nations and people. The books are basically grammar- and writing-centred although, *First things First* says about itself that it is aimed at training students in the four skills, which did not prove to be true in my eyes.

The reader can find few illustrations, these are rather impersonal drawings than pictures or photographs, which present no otherness. (For instance in *First Things First* there are only eight pages among 146, on which we can meet colourful pictures.) The photographs are mostly about objects and buildings, not about people. In spite of these facts such books were considered to be effective and suitable for teaching a foreign language, as *Success with English* was also called a "modern, fully illustrated" material.

2. The seventies

The books that I have analysed are:

- L.G. Alexander (1973) Mainline Progress

Longman, London

- B. Abbs - I. Freebairn (1977) Starting Strategies

Longman, London

- B. Abbs - I- Freebairn (1979) Building Strategies

Longman, London

In the 1970s the multicultural aspect appears in the textbooks, although it does not penetrate the whole course. There are texts about more interesting and peculiar topics, like marriage ceremonies of different people in *Mainline Progress* or Life in the 21st century in *Building Strategies.* The appearance of semi-authentic and authentic materials is a big advantage of these books. The one from 1979 also introduced some literature into foreign language teaching. The exercises are more varied (like "identify yourself" in Alexander's book), there are pair works, moreover, students have a chance to discuss problematic questions as well. The books are more picturesque, we can find more illustrations and photographs about otherness as well, although, pictures about black people only appear in the book towards the end of the decade. Despite the fact that there are more piquancy and peculiarities, in my opinion, the background information about other cultures provided by these language books is still not sufficient.

3. The eighties

I have examined:

- A. doff - L. Jones - K. Mitchell (1983) Meanings into words
Cambridge University Press

- R. Kingsbury - G. Wellman (1986) Longman Advanced English
Longman, London

- D.R. Levine - J. Baxter - P. McNulty (1987) The Culture Puzzle
Prentice Hall Resents

- P. Buckley - L. Prodromou (1988) On the Move
Oxford University Press

- S. Dalzell - I. Edgar (1988) English in Perspective
Oxford University Press

At this time the intercultural aspect is not only present but by the and of the decade it is one of the determinative factors of coursebooks. More types of people, characters and ways of life are presented with the help of both pictures and texts, however, there are still not too many pictures about minorities, like blacks.

More and more authentic and semi-authentic materials are built in the syllabus, for example, newspapers play an important role, especially in *On the Move.* There is always a possibility for students to express their own opinions about politics, social issues, trends etc. In the scope of role plays as well. In the book from 1986 significant topics appear, like first impressions, differences between nationalities, while the book from 1983 is still dealing with rather universal issues, like "Has the quality of life improved in the last 50 years?"

The *Culture Puzzle* is an exception among these books, a speciality, which I have chosen to prove the fact that there have already been new ways, trials in the 80s to teach a foreign language from a totally multicultural point of view.

4. The nineties

The books from the 90s are:

- J. Harmer - R. Rossner (1991) More than Words

Longman, London

- T. Hutchinson (1991) Hotline

Oxford University Press

- R. Nolasco (1991) WOW! Window on the World

Oxford University Press

- L. Woolcott (1994) First Choice

Prentice Hall International Ltd

While I was examining these books I had the feeling that here multiculturalism is not only a supplementary or additional issue to foreign language teaching, but a guiding force that influences this whole process. There are not only playful, interesting tasks ("imagine" tasks, role plays, describing a person in a photo in a positive/negative way) but thought-provoking topics as well about prejudices, stereotyping, vandalism, women's rights or multi-ethnic societies. In *WOW!* There is a text about an experimentation, when a class was divided into blue-eyed and brown-eyed students and one group was superior to the other. This is also a good example of raising aggression and discrimination and also a deterrence from behaving similarly. In my opinion, it is very useful that these books try to mingle music, literature and language to a higher degree because they are also representatives of a certain culture. It does not have to be mentioned that these materials are very picturesque, colourful - like the world we live in - and people from other cultural backgrounds are not only presented, as specialities, but they have significant roles (for example Casey and Kamala in *Hotline*).

I have also found an interesting book from 2001, its title is *Cultural Relations* (P. Károly - Sz. Ildikó - J. Daniella - S. Ferenc - S. Emőke). It attracted my attention because it teaches not only language but historical, political, social, geographical, and cultural knowledge about English speaking countries too. In spite of the fact that it is not a "conventional" coursebook, it may set an example to future textbooks how to alloy language teaching with other - sometimes problematical - fields of life.

V.3. Summary

Taking all things into consideration, it can be pointed out that during the decades, since language teachers became more and more experienced, the theory and practice of foreign language teaching improved a lot. As linguistics, pedagogy and sociology were interwoven, books were brought to perfection. Nevertheless, nothing can be called "perfect" or "ready", the process of improvement will never stop. After the intercultural aspect has already been introduced into books, our most important task is to "plant" it into the heads of teachers and students as well. We may have the best coursebooks to teach from but without a right way of thinking and attitude we cannot achieve our purposes.

CONCLUSION

What would be a world like in which there were no differences and otherness, in which we could find similar people with similar cultures, living in the same way? Disparities and contrasts give our world a furtherance, still people are often too blind and self-centred to appreciate this feature of life. The shameful periods of our history will always stand as warning examples in front of the human race. If we do not want them to repeat themselves, we have to overcome the small-mindedness, the fear of otherness, the prejudices, which can be found in every one of us to a certain degree.

Bringing up a child is always a great responsibility. We must prepare them for life physically and psychologically as well and, as I have mentioned before, it is not only the duty of the parents, but of the teachers and educational institutes too. In both roles we must be worthy for the children's attention, esteem and trust. Fortunately, nowadays the multicultural aspect of teaching is occupying its right place - at least in theory - but if we look around us, there are still plenty of problems (discrimination, racism, xenophobia...) that should be dealt with, that must be solved.

This cannot be done by one person, it has to be done by everybody, by our whole race, joining hands and forces. It is going to be a long and exhausting process but the first steps have already been taken. The new generation, our children and grandchildren, are going to carry on this way, for that reason, we must help them to get acquainted with otherness, so that they will not be afraid of it.

Different races, colours, different religions or ethnic groups - all are secondary issues, the main thing is that we are human beings, all of the same kind. With the right way of thinking, with the help of multicultural view, we can become acquainted with a multicoloured world.

-40-

BIBLIOGRAPHY

- Bárdos, J. (1997) A nyelvtanítás története és a módszerfogalom tartalma
Veszprémi Egyetemi Kiadó, Veszprém

- Brander, P. - Cardenas, C. - Gomes, R. - Taylor, M. - de Vicente Abad, J. (1995) All different/All equal education pack (Ideas, resources, methods and activities for informal intercultural education with young people and adults)
Council of Europe, Strasbourg

- Brander, P. - Cardenas, C. - Gomes, R. - Taylor, M. - de Vicente Abad, J. (1996) Domino (A manual to use peer group education as a means to fight racism, xenophobia, anti-semitism and intolerance)
Council of Europe, Strasbourg

- Byram, M. - Tost Planet, M. (2000) Social Identity and the European Dimension: Intercultural Competence Through Foreign Language Learning
Council of Europe Publishing, Germany

- Dr. Kühn Jánosné (1997) Találkozások - Interkulturális nevelés IV. (Óraleírások, oktatócsomagok és projektek gyűjteménye különböző népek kultúráiról)
Pax Christi, Szeged

- Fenner, A.B. (2001) Cultural awareness and language awareness based on dialogic interaction with texts in foreign language learning
Council of Europe, Germany

- Garton, A. F. (1992) Social Interaction and the Development of Language and Cognition
Lawrence Earlbaum Associates, Hove/Hillsday

- Goldman, L. - Poór, Z. (1999) Európai Dimenziók a Hazai Nyelvoktatásban
Tallér Kiadó, Veszprém

- Merrill Valdes, J. (1986) Culture Bound
Cambridge University Press, USA

Wissenschaftlicher Buchverlag bietet

kostenfreie

Publikation

von

wissenschaftlichen Arbeiten

Diplomarbeiten, Magisterarbeiten, Master und Bachelor Theses
sowie Dissertationen, Habilitationen und wissenschaftliche Monographien

e verfügen über eine wissenschaftliche Abschlußarbeit zu aktuellen oder zeitlosen
Fragestellungen, die hohen inhaltlichen und formalen Ansprüchen genügt,
und haben **Interesse an einer honorarvergüteten Publikation**?

Dann senden Sie bitte erste Informationen über Ihre Arbeit per Email
an info@vdm-verlag.de. Unser Außenlektorat meldet sich umgehend bei Ihnen.

VDM Verlag Dr. Müller Aktiengesellschaft & Co. KG
Dudweiler Landstraße 125a
D - 66123 Saarbrücken

www.vdm-verlag.de